Mpowered Me presents

Mindset Reset

Unlock the Power of Transformation

BY

NATASHA RICHARDS

Watersprings
PUBLISHING

Mindset Reset by Natasha Richards
Published by Watersprings Publishing,
a division of Watersprings Media House, LLC.
P.O. Box 1284 Olive Branch, MS 38654
www.waterspringspublishing.com

Contact the publisher for bulk orders and permission requests.

Printed in the United States of America.

Scripture quotations credited to ERV are taken from the Holy Bible: Easy-to-Read Version (ERV), International Edition © 2013, 2016 by Bible League International and used by permission.

Scripture quotations credited to NASB are from the *New American Standard Bible*, copyright © 1960, 1962, 1963, 1968, 1971, 1972, 1973, 1975, by the Lockman Foundation. Used by permission.

ISBN-13: 979-8-9859594-8-2

CONTENTS

Introduction

Congratulations on taking the first step towards a more empowered life with Mpowered Me. It takes a lot of courage to make this decision, and I'm proud of you for taking this step. The journey ahead may bring up some difficult emotions, and if you ever feel overwhelmed, it's okay to take a break and seek professional counseling. Remember that you're not alone, and when you're ready, we can continue on this journey together towards a better and stronger you.

Mpowered Me was designed to guide you toward developing a positive and powerful mindset to become the best version of yourself. We understand that this journey may bring up some difficult emotions or experiences, but please know that we are here to support you every step of the way. We recommend that you confide in someone you trust and ask for their prayers as you embark on this transformative journey. Remember to be patient with yourself and trust the process. We will equip you with the necessary tools to enhance your life and reach your full potential.

It's not uncommon for many Christians to face difficulty when considering going to a professional therapist. The question that often arises is, "Why can't my spiritual relationship with Jesus be enough?" However, it's essential to understand your emotions and decision-making process before your spiritual relationship can truly make sense. We all know that Jesus is the ultimate guide, but applying biblical principles to our lives can sometimes be challenging. I sincerely hope the Mpowered Me books and program can assist you in this journey.

Please keep in mind that our books and programs are intended to be used as a complement to therapy, not a replacement for it. You may encounter challenging emotions and memories as you progress through our materials. If this occurs, we strongly advise you to seek the assistance of a trained therapist. Our resources are designed to enhance your journey towards healing, not substitute it.

Achieving success in this program requires using *The Journal Workbook* in conjunction with this book. While reading is vital for acquiring knowledge, journaling enables you to solidify your comprehension, and the workbook provides opportunities for practical application. Following these three steps will empower you to achieve a positive transformation. To truly succeed in this journey, it is crucial to have someone who will support and hold you accountable. This person will pray for you as you navigate the program and ensure you remain committed to the tactical steps necessary for success.

In this book, you will be encouraged to study scripture as it relates to the topic of discovery. We will use the SOAP method to do so.

Using the SOAP according to The Salvation Army:

S – Scripture – Read a short Bible passage out loud. (I will give specific scripture for each topic.)

O – Observation – What do you notice about the verse? What do you think the main message is? What verses, words, or ideas jump out to you?

A – Application – Ask God how he wants you to apply the verse to your life.

P – Prayer – Pray for yourself and/or for others.

As you embark on this journey, know that my prayers are with you. May you witness the transformative power of God's hand in your life. The Journal Workbook will provide a solid foundation for your work, using the scriptures as your guide. Achieve your spiritual goals by dedicating a week to each specific topic. Begin by reading and meditating on relevant scripture, and then utilize The Journal Workbook to follow through on your reflections.

Romans 12:2 (NIV)
*"Do not conform to the pattern of this world, but
be transformed by the renewing of your mind. Then
you will be able to test and approve what God's will
is—his good, leasing and perfect will."*

01
DAMAGED GOODS

"This was the Lord's first message to Hosea. The Lord said, "Go, marry a prostitute who has had children as a result of her prostitution." (Hosea 1:2, ESV)

"All damaged people are dangerous. Survival makes them so. 'Why?' Because they have no pity. They know what others can survive, as they did." – Josephine Hart, Damage

I believe it is possible to make a strong case that the wife of the prophet Hosea was emotionally damaged. I don't say this because she was a prostitute. I say this because the prophet Hosea, under the instruction of God, took her and made her his wife. This was meant to illustrate the mercy of God that was available to the Israelites. She was given a way out of this situation, yet she chose to return to prostitution.

I'm making some assumptions here. I assume that she now finds herself in a functional relationship. I assume that she is with a good and godly man who understands that a good man loves his wife as much as, if not more than he loves himself. I assume she is loved and treated well and was not abused or mistreated by the prophet.

Here, you have someone who has an opportunity to be loved, cherished, and protected, yet she returns to what she knows best. She goes back to a life of sexual objectification. She goes back to a life where her body is used for the gratification of unknown numbers of men. **She goes back to what feels familiar.** For emotionally challenged people, dysfunction can feel comfortable and even appropriate.

This is what makes helping someone who is emotionally damaged a challenging undertaking. This is because there is a level of emotional complexity and a lack of awareness of how their behavior and actions impact the people who care about them.

Damaged individuals exhibit many of the following behaviors: an inability to trust others, or offer and receive physical expressions of love; they may exhibit a lack of self-confidence and low self-esteem; they may experience feelings of depression, despair, and hopelessness, and may have recurring thoughts of death and dying. In an attempt to self-medicate, many individuals who are emotionally damaged turn to alcohol and drugs as a means of coping with reality.

There are two essential things to remember. **First, do not enable that individual to continue his or her behavior.** Be a friend, and encourage them, but don't get sucked into their drama. Don't validate their faulty thinking by agreeing with their destructive life patterns.

Second, do not try to fix damaged individuals or their

problems. Until someone reaches a place where they recognize they have a problem and desire to find a solution, trying to fix them or their problem will only result in frustration.

But what if that damaged person is you? What if you have had a hurtful experience or relationship that has caused you to lose trust in others, made you fearful of allowing others to get close to you, or resulted in you having mean behaviors to others?

Perhaps you are afraid to try something new -- beginning a new relationship, looking for a new job, moving to a new city -- because you know what you feel now or the experience you are in now. Still, you need to know or have a guarantee that taking a chance will work. Like Hosea's wife, you are drawn to what you know and what feels comfortable.

If you have been hurt by life's circumstances or individuals that have passed through your life, remember that you are not alone. Recognize that these problems, although difficult, will not kill you. You can win this battle. Make up your mind that you will not let what happened damage you emotionally. Decide to stretch yourself because growth comes through stretching yourself. And don't wait until tomorrow to begin; start today.

MPOWERED ME NEXT STEPS

S – Scripture – Read Hosea 1:1-7 out loud.

O – Observation – What do you notice about the verses? What do you think the main message is? What verses, words, or ideas jump out to you?

A – Application – Ask God how he wants you to apply the verse to your life.

P – Prayer – Pray for yourself and/or for others.

Chapter Reflection: Damaged Goods

_____

_____

_____

_____

_____

_____

To go deeper into this topic, please refer to **The Journal Workbook**.

02

THE VIEW I SEE

Then Mephibosheth the [a]*grandson of Saul came down to meet the king; but he had neither* [b]*tended to his feet, nor [c]trimmed his mustache, nor washed his clothes since the day the king departed until the day he came home in peace. (2 Sam. 19:24, NASB)*

"Sometimes we underestimate ourselves so much that when people compliment us, we can never believe them."
-- www.livelifehappy.com

Mephibosheth had a royal bloodline. He was the grandson of Saul, king of Israel, and the son of Jonathan, the son of Saul. Both his father and grandfather died when he was five years of age. It was customary to kill the remaining lineage to ensure that no one could reclaim the throne, but he escaped. His nurse tried to flee with him to save his life, she picked him up, but in her rush, he fell and became crippled.

You can imagine how he must feel. He was an heir to the throne that was now crippled. It would've been easier if he had been born cripple, but he was born fully capable of functioning, like every other boy his age. Now he is crippled. The things he used to do on his own now must be completed with the assistance of others. He felt embarrassed, and he felt unworthy. He was no longer independent. His self-esteem dropped, and he no longer acted like the royalty that he was.

Here is the sad part: even though Mephibosheth was now crippled, he was still heir to the throne and could have claimed what he was rightfully entitled to receive at any time. The problem was he associated with his disability more than he did his identity; he was still a prince. When you look at the actions, you recognize that they were less than princely. It wasn't his disability that disqualified him from still receiving royal treatment; it was his mindset.

When David discovered that an heir of Saul was being managed in such a terrible fashion, he ordered that henceforth, Mephibosheth would forever have a seat at the king's table. Yet, because he saw himself as a cripple, he responded from his disability and not from the power and authority of his birthright. David tried to elevate him, but he should not have needed elevation. Although he was Saul's grandson and Jonathan's son, he could not see what David saw in him. When he looked at himself, he saw a cripple, not a prince.

Think about how many times others have tried to elevate or compliment you, and you could not accept or receive what they were giving because the mirror you used to view yourself did not reflect what you were hearing. I submit to you that if this happens often, the mirror you use is faulty; you need to ditch that mirror and find another mirror.

Ask yourself, "Why do I view myself so negatively?" Sometimes, it comes from the things others have said to you in the past. Reject those thoughts. You are not who others say you are. You are who God says you are. And God says you are someone special. Remember that whenever someone seeks to elevate you or offers you a compliment, it shines a light on a positive act, quality, or personal character trait.

MPOWERED ME NEXT STEPS

S – Scripture – Read 2 Samuel 19:16-24 out loud.
O – Observation – What do you notice about the verses? What do you think the main message is? What verses, words, or ideas jump out to you?
A – Application – Ask God how he wants you to apply the verse to your life.
P – Prayer – Pray for yourself and/or for others.

Chapter Reflection: The View I See

_____

_____

_____

_____

_____

_____

_____

To go deeper into this topic, please refer to **The Journal Workbook**.

03

THE ANGER WITHIN

My dear brothers and sisters, always be more willing
to listen than to speak. Keep control of your anger.
20 Anger does not help you live the way God wants.
(James 1:19-20, ERV)

"Holding on to anger is like grasping a hot coal with the intent
of throwing it at someone else; you are the one who gets
burned." -- Buddha

Anger is a reaction when someone experiences a situation or is the target of an action that leaves them feeling vulnerable, unfairly criticized, irritated, frustrated, defenseless, help-less, unappreciated, mistreated, or disrespected. It is an individualized emotion because everyone does not respond the same way to every trigger. That is why you may find yourself angered by something that impacts another person differently or not at all.

Many factors influence how we respond to the various triggers. Sometimes, it concerns the messages you received in childhood about anger and the proper way to express it. This could involve the acceptance, by others, of the anger you expressed growing up or witnessing how those around you express anger.

Other times, it has to do with your experiences that caused you to experience anger. These situations may involve abuse, being bullied, or going through a traumatic experience. As a result, you are challenged when faced with certain situations or experience specific actions. You are reminded of what happened to you in the past that you have not resolved, and the anger reflects what you have not resolved about the past.

It can also have to do with what is currently happening in your life. You feel overwhelmed with problems that you have no control over. You don't like how someone else is behaving toward you. Your life is not developing in the way that you wish it would. Or it could be so many other things. Something in your life leaves you feeling frustrated, exasperated, helpless, and wronged. That might result in feelings of anger that you would not ordinarily experience.

The reality is that there are better solutions than anger for most problems. It is not a productive way to address your situation and will likely make things worse. When you are angry, consider taking these steps instead of acting out.

Count to ten before you speak or react. In fact, it is probably a good idea not to speak or react at all while you are angry. Once you say a hurtful word or engage in hateful actions, you won't be able to take those things back if you realize later that you overreacted, or worse, you misunderstood or were in the wrong but didn't have the facts correctly. Slow yourself down and force yourself to wait the anger out; you will never regret not acting out in anger.

Take time to think about what happened and assess your role in causing it to happen, if any. In most situations, you will play some part in what happened, even if it is a small part. You cannot take responsibility for what others do; however, you can take responsibility for your actions. Be prepared to have a conversation with the individual or individuals involved, let them know what they have done that hurts you, and be willing to admit the part that you played in the situation.

When the anger subsides, express your feelings in an assertively and nonconfrontationally. Choosing to wait your anger out is not the same as ignoring the problem or sweeping it under the rug. Issues don't go away on their own; they must be dealt with. However, when addressing the situation with others, make the situation the problem and not the people involved. That means thinking through what you will say and then saying it in a way that is not hurtful, manipulative, or controlling.

Don't hold a grudge. If you have dealt with it, and everyone involved understands each other and agrees to forgive and move forward, LET IT GO! Understand that forgiveness is not about the other person. Forgiveness is about freeing yourself from negative feelings, hurt, and pain.
American novelist Anne Lamott said it best: *"Not forgiving is like drinking rat poison and then waiting for the rat to die."* Let it go. Can it be that easy? It's not easy. You can choose not to act. Choose to master your anger; don't let your anger master you. That is one ingredient to a happy life.

MPOWERED ME NEXT STEPS

S – Scripture – Read James 1:12-19 out loud.

O – Observation – What do you notice about the verses? What do you think the main message is? What verses, words, or ideas jump out to you?

A – Application – Ask God how he wants you to apply the verse to your life.

P – Prayer – Pray for yourself and/or for others.

Chapter Reflection: The Anger Within

_____

_____

_____

_____

_____

_____

To go deeper into this topic, please refer to **The Journal Workbook**.

04

FORGIVENESS FOR REAL

"Then Joseph said to them, "Don't be afraid. I am not God! I have no right to punish you. It is true that you planned to do something bad to me. But really, God was planning good things. God's plan was to use me to save the lives of many people. And that is what happened. So don't be afraid. I will take care of you and your children." And so Joseph said kind things to his brothers, and this made them feel better." (Genesis 50:19-21, ERV)

"I am thankful for all those difficult people in my life, they have shown me exactly who I do not want to be."
–Kushandwizoom

One of the hardest things to do in life is forgive those who intentionally cause you hurt. Although the results are often very painful, it is easier to continue having relationships with individuals who cause unintentional pain, and it is much more challenging to continue engaging and interacting in the same way as before. It is hard to maintain the same relationship when that person knows what they are about to do will hurt or harm you, yet they did it anyway.

Part of the reason forgiveness is so difficult is a misunderstanding of what forgiveness is and what forgiveness does. When you forgive, it doesn't mean that you are saying the other person is not wrong. It doesn't mean that you are sweeping it under the rug or pretending it isn't a problem or that it wasn't wrong, and it doesn't mean that you are not justified in the anger you feel. If that is your view of forgiveness, forgiving will be difficult.

In reality, forgiveness is more about you than the other person. When you forgive, you are letting go of your hurt, wounds, resentments, and grudges so that you can focus on more productive things. Forgiveness brings about closure and allows you to move on and choose joy. When you forgive, you regain control of your emotions, and you can now resume the relationship on any terms you desire.

We have the example of Joseph as he dealt with his brothers. His father died, and there was nothing to keep him from exacting vengeance upon the brothers who tried to kill him and then sold him into slavery. What they didn't understand is the power of God's plan in the life of those who trust him. When they sold him to the caravan headed for Egypt, they set into motion a chain of events that led to the fulfillment of Joseph's dreams.

When all is set and done, forgiveness more easily comes when you trust in the power of God to take the bad that others do to you and use the circumstance that occurs to bless your life. You have a choice: you can complain and stay angry, bitter, and resentful at the people who hurt you, or trust God, forgive, and allow him to lead you on your journey.

MPOWERED ME NEXT STEPS

S – Scripture – Read Genesis 50:15-20 out loud.

O – Observation – What do you notice about the verses? What do you think the main message is? What verses, words, or ideas jump out to you?

A – Application – Ask God how he wants you to apply the verse to your life.

P – Prayer – Pray for yourself and/or for others.

Chapter Reflection: The Forgiveness For Real

_____

_____

_____

_____

_____

_____

To go deeper into this topic, please refer to **The Journal Workbook. ****

Philippians 4:8 (NIV):
"Finally, brothers and sisters, whatever is true, whatever is noble, whatever is right, whatever is pure, whatever is lovely, whatever is admirable—if anything is excellent or praiseworthy—think about such things."

05

A MASK

¹⁴Curse the day that I was born! Don't bless the day my mother had me. ¹⁵Curse the man who told my father the news that I was born. "It's a boy!" he said. "You have a son." . . . . ¹⁷If he had killed me, then my mother would have been my grave, and I would not have been born. ¹⁸Why did I have to come out of her body? All I have seen is trouble and sorrow, and my life will end in shame.
(Jeremiah 20:14-15, 17-18, ERV)

"Sometimes when I say, 'I'm okay,' I want someone to look me in the eyes, hug me tight and say, 'I know you're not.'"
– Unknown

The prophet Jeremiah had intense insecurity, loneliness, and low self-esteem. He battled depression. In fact, he is called the "weeping prophet." He was rejected by the people to whom he ministered. However, he was not allowed to marry and have children and lived a life of poverty. He lived life alone and felt like a failure. He could have used a little comfort, a hug, affirmation, and encouragement. There were many times when seeing a smile would've made a significant difference in his life.

Depression occurs more often than we know. Part of the difficulty in identifying a depressed person happens because although many signs are readily evident, other symptoms are not as obvious. We recognize the common expressions: sadness and feeling down, crying, and feeling helpless and hopeless. However, depression can also manifest in fatigue and low energy, loss of desire to eat, lack of interest in being intimate with loved ones, and physical aches and pains that happen for no reason.

Depression can even lead to thoughts of suicide or harming oneself. Recently I responded to an individual on a social media page, who wanted to give up. Later, I read the feed, and others also responded. We affirmed his feelings and encouraged him not to give up and reach out for help. Weeks later, he is still on social media and is thankful for the love and support given to him through social media; many of these people he never even met.

Hearing that someone cares about him and what happens to him kept him from ending his life. It doesn't cost anything to be kind. It doesn't cost anything to encourage. Letting someone know you care what happens to them doesn't cost anything. Sometimes, all it takes is a smile, hug, or words of affirmation. You may never know what being too nice to someone might mean to him or her.

You may look at someone who seems happy, yet behind the mask is someone who could use comfort and would love to be hugged, affirmed, and encouraged. You might see someone who needs to see a smile. Wearing a smile requires fewer muscles than it does to frown. A smile is an excellent therapy for you and those who come in contact with you. Smile even if it is because you woke up this morning and for the small things in life. Smile because it might just make a difference in someone else's life.

The 988 Lifeline provides 24/7, confidential support to people in suicidal crisis or mental health-related distress. By calling or texting 988, you'll connect to mental health professionals with the Lifeline network.

MPOWERED ME NEXT STEPS

S – Scripture – Read Jeremiah 20 out loud.

O – Observation – What do you notice about the verses? What do you think the main message is? What verses, words, or ideas jump out to you?

A – Application – Ask God how he wants you to apply the verse to your life.

P – Prayer – Pray for yourself and/or for others.

Chapter Reflection: A Mask

_____

_____

_____

_____

_____

_____

To go deeper into this topic, please refer to **The Journal Workbook**.

06

REACTION

Jonah was not happy that God saved the city. Jonah became angry. ²He complained to the LORD and said, "LORD, I knew this would happen! I was in my own country, and you told me to come here. At that time I knew that you would forgive the people of this evil city, so I decided to run away to Tarshish. I knew that you are a kind God. I knew that you show mercy and don't want to punish people. I knew that you are kind, and if these people stopped sinning, you would change your plans to destroy them. ³ So now, LORD, just kill me. It is better for me to die than to live."
(Jonah 4:1-3, ERV)

"We often add to our pain and suffering by being overly sensitive, over-reacting to minor things, and sometimes taking things too personally." – Dalai Lama

Have you ever looked back at a situation and realized that you overreacted or were overly sensitive? Have you ever reacted to a situation and recognized that you might not have gone a little overboard after you had time to cool down and wished you could take things back or do things over? This is what happened to Jonah. God sent him to preach a message of repentance to the people of Nineveh, *"After 40 days, Nineveh would be destroyed." (Jonah 3:4, ERV)*

Jonah refused to go to Nineveh and took a boat headed in the opposite direction. God allowed a storm to occur that threatened to rock the boat. When the men on the ship found out that Jonah's presence on the vessel was the reason for the storm, they eventually tossed him into the sea. God sent a big fish to rescue Jonah. Jonah repented while inside the fish, and God directed the fish to vomit Jonah onto dry land.

God gave Jonah a do-over. Jonah went to Nineveh and preached the message God gave him. The people of Nineveh repent after hearing Jonah, and God relents from destroying the city. However, Jonah is so angry that he asks God to take his life. Why? Probably because he is worried that the people will begin to call him a false prophet. He said Nineveh would be destroyed in 40 days, 40 days have now come and gone, and Nineveh is still intact. Jonah overreacted. There are times when everyone overreacts. There are some things we can do to minimize overreacting in life.

First, **recognize that every reaction is not necessarily an overreaction.** We are created to have emotions. At times, you will experience righteous anger. At times, you will have moments of intense sadness and crying. At times, you will rightfully sever a relationship with a toxic person in your life. However, learn to recognize situations where using a mallet is much more appropriate than using a sledgehammer.

Second, **identify the people or things that trigger you to overreact.** You can probably identify things that set us off and the people who know how to push our buttons. Make a conscious effort to exert self-control when you are around these people or facing those situations. The fact is, no one can make you overreact; overreacting is a choice you make. You could choose not to overreact and walk away or ignore.

Third, **think before you speak or act around these people or things that trigger you to overreact.** Whatever it is you need to do -- count to 100, take a deep breath, walk away, go for a drive or bicycle ride – when you feel that you are likely to or about to overreact, leave the situation. You might be able to apologize for an action or harsh words, but you will never be able to take it back. Don't say it or do it unless you are going to be okay with whatever outcome you experience.

Fourth, **figure out why you are reacting in this way.** What makes you jump or feel angry when a particular person is near you? Why are you unable to respond positively when in a specific situation? Why do you continually say no to attempts by someone to befriend you? Why is it that when certain things happen or certain people are around, you start feeling negative emotions? Figuring out why is the first step to solving the problem of overreacting.

MPOWERED ME NEXT STEPS

S – Scripture – Read Jonah 3 out loud.
O – Observation – What do you notice about the verses? What do you think the main message is? What verses, words, or ideas jump out to you?
A – Application – Ask God how he wants you to apply the verse to your life.
P – Prayer – Pray for yourself and/or for others.

Chapter Reflection: Reaction

_____

_____

_____

_____

_____

_____

To go deeper into this topic, please refer to **The Journal Workbook**.

07

ON MY SIDE

When they saw him from a distance and before he came close to them, they plotted against him to put him to death. They said to one another, "Here comes this dreamer! Now then, come and let us kill him and throw him into one of the pits, and we will say, 'A wild beast devoured him.' Then let us see what will become of his dreams." (Genesis 37:18-20, NASB)

"Not everyone will appreciate what you do for them. You have to figure out who's worth your kindness and who's just taking advantage." – Unknown

It must have been incredibly challenging for Joseph to find himself in a situation where his own siblings were plotting against him. Despite being sent by his father to assist them, they harbored resentment towards his leadership ambitions and intended to cause him harm. Nevertheless, Joseph's unwavering perseverance and belief in his vision serve as a powerful reminder to us all to never give up on our dreams, even when faced with adversity.

When you achieve success, it's crucial to be aware that not everyone will be happy for you. Take time to reflect on those you confide in and assess the people in your life. Ask yourself if they genuinely have your best interests at heart, as only some people want to see you succeed.

You will encounter friends who will celebrate your achievements and support you in life. However, there will also be individuals who will have negative attitudes and malicious intentions towards you. It is essential to maintain a distance from such people as their negativity can have a detrimental impact on your life and even lead to betrayal. It is best to cherish relationships with those who encourage and inspire you while avoiding those who bring you down.

The prophet Isaiah gave us wise counsel when he said, *"Don't put your trust in mere humans. They are frail as breath. What good are they?" (Isaiah 2:22, NLT)*

No matter how well you know someone and no matter how much they love you, they are prone to disappoint you from time to time, and they are likely to fail you at a time when you need them the most. That is a painful experience. Here is a quote that sums it up nicely. It says, "Nothing hurts more than being disappointed [or betrayed] by the person you thought would never hurt you." (Unknown Author)

So, what do you do when you've been betrayed? Here are some recommendations:

Allow yourself to feel the hurt and grief, but don't wallow forever. It is important to acknowledge that what happened hurt. Allowing yourself to grieve healthily (cry, scream, comfort food) is even good. Set yourself a timeline (I allow myself 24 hours), then I continue to live my life. You don't need to wait for your emotions to change before you act the way you are when you are happy. If you decide that I will act happy and do what I would ordinarily do if I were happy, your emotions will follow, and then you will be happy. It takes a lot of practice and intentional implementation in your life.

Give yourself permission to move on. Stop dwelling on what was done to you. Don't spend time looking for evidence of cosmic retribution – i.e., what goes around comes around. Cease from the continual replay of what happened and what you should've done differently. Accept that you do not deserve the bad experiences of what happened to you. Understand that you are not a fool. Choose to be happy and emotionally healthy and do those things that will bring you to that state of being. Just make up your mind that "I am moving on." Choose you! This is not about being a good Christian or a good person. This is about your health.

Learn to forgive the one who betrayed you. Someone once compared holding on to your hurt and refusing to forgive those who hurt you to drinking something poisonous and expecting it to hurt the other person. The only person who will be hurt is you. When you forgive the one who has disappointed or betrayed you, you give yourself a gift. It doesn't mean that you must forget what happens. It also doesn't mean you must allow that person back into your life. You are freeing yourself to be fully healed.

The question you should ask is, what is forgiveness? When you learn what this is, it will help you move forward positively in your process.

Don't allow your treatment of others to be clouded by this betrayal. Everyone deserves to be treated based on what they do and not what someone else has not done. If someone says something or does something that causes you to relive the betrayal or the person who betrays you, take a deep breath before you react. They are not who betrayed you and should not be treated as if they were. Be honest and explain why you are so bothered by what happened. One betrayal doesn't mean there isn't anyone out there who is worthy of your trust.

MPOWERED ME NEXT STEPS

S – Scripture – Read Genesis 37:1-18 out loud.

O – Observation – What do you notice about the verses? What do you think the main message is? What verses, words, or ideas jump out to you?

A – Application – Ask God how he wants you to apply the verse to your life.

P – Prayer – Pray for yourself and/or for others.

Chapter Reflection: On My Side

_____

_____

_____

_____

_____

_____

To go deeper into this topic, please refer to **The Journal Workbook**.

2 Corinthians 10:5 (NIV):
"We demolish arguments and every pretension that sets itself up against the knowledge of God, and we take captive every thought to make it obedient to Christ."

08

COMMON MISTAKE

Great blessings belong to those who suffer persecution for doing what is right. God's kingdom belongs to them. People will insult you and hurt you. They will lie and say all kinds of evil things about you because you follow me. But when they do that, know that great blessings belong to you. Be happy about it. Be very glad because you have a great reward waiting for you in heaven. People did these same things to the prophets who lived before you.
(Matthew 5:10-12, ERV))

"The true mark of maturity is when somebody hurts you and you try to understand their situation instead of trying to hurt them back." –Ryron Gracie

A common mistake many people make is holding on to feelings of hurt. It doesn't make sense when you think about it; you are the one who hurts the most. Many times, if not most of the time, the one who has hurt you is not thinking about what they have done to you, is not aware that you are still affected by the hurt they caused you, and quite often, they don't care about how you're feeling.

Author Anne Lamott says it well, "In fact, forgiving is like drinking rat poison and then waiting for the rat to die." Hurt is a feeling that can cause unspeakable pain that tears into your soul daily. If the hurt is not released, it can cause heart attacks, strokes, migraines, ulcers, and other ailments. This is just a list of the physical effects; the hurt can also result in a mental breakdown.

The best way to deal with hurt is to accept a fact stated in an unknown author's quote, "pain is inevitable, but suffering is optional." When I have been hurt by someone else, I put myself in the other person's shoes and try to understand the situation from their perspective. Doing this allows me to forgive. Once I forgive, I let it go and chalk it to something done by someone who doesn't know better. It doesn't excuse the situation but allows me to put things in perspective and move on.

In dealing with hurt, you **must not allow yourself to be guided by your emotions**. Acting out while being led by your feelings rarely results in a good decision. Instead, step back, let your emotions settle down, and wait to decide until you have a clear mind. Removing yourself from contact with this person or the situation causing hurt may be necessary. When your mind is clear, you can be more objective in your assessment of the situation and better assess whether you are responding from your emotions, and you are more likely to make a decision that you don't regret later on.

Once you have allowed your emotions to settle and your mind is clear, **move to a place of resolution.** To reach this place, you need to connect with the person who caused you to hurt, express your feelings of hurt in a non-accusatory way, and see if your hurt is a result of an explainable misunderstanding. Approach the conversation with an open mind and a willingness to understand the other person's perspective. Be measured and thoughtful with the words you use.

Decide the path you take with this person or circumstance moving forward. Decide on where this relationship is going. Forgiveness does not necessarily equate to having the same connection or the same interactions. Recognize when it is best to part company, yet have no hard feelings, nor hold a grudge. On the other hand, if you decide that things will remain as is, you cannot continue bringing up what happened. Give yourself permission to release that part of the past.

MPOWERED ME NEXT STEPS

S – Scripture – Read Matthew 5:1-12 out loud.

O – Observation – What do you notice about the verses? What do you think the main message is? What verses, words, or ideas jump out to you?

A – Application – Ask God how he wants you to apply the verse to your life.

P – Prayer – Pray for yourself and/or for others.

Chapter Reflection: Common Mistake

_____

_____

_____

_____

_____

_____

To go deeper into this topic, please refer to **The Journal Workbook**.

09

DRAMA

Great blessings belong to those who don't listen to evil advice, who don't live like sinners, and who don't join those who make fun of God. Instead, they love the Lord's teachings and think about them day and night. So they grow strong, like a tree planted by a stream— a tree that produces fruit when it should and has leaves that never fall. Everything they do is successful. (Psalm 1:1-3, ERV)

"There comes a time in your life when you walk away from all the drama and people who create it. You surround yourself with people who make you laugh. Forget the bad and focus on the good. Love the people who treat you right, pray for the ones who do not. Life is too short to be anything but happy. Falling down is a part of life, getting back up is living."
— José N. Harris

I have lived long enough to recognize that some people don't know or perhaps don't appreciate the joy of enjoying a peaceful life. They constantly go through life from crisis to crisis and drama to drama. They are forever caught up in some problem. And when there is no problem, they create a situation that qualifies as an emergency or a catastrophe.

You may know someone who fits this description. Everything seems to be out of control. Something is always going on that is so bad that they must share it with others. They enjoy calling people and seeking assistance in resolving the drama and fixing the crisis, yet it is usually clear that they are the leading cause of all that crisis and drama.

Psychologists categorize these behaviors as being one of several personality disorders in what they call "Cluster B." These are people who can't seem to get through life without some form of crisis or drama. They make a big deal about what would be a minor problem to others. They exaggerate the intensity of the problem. What is worse is they may drag you into their drama and find a reason why you are the reason for their current situation.

How do you deal with an individual who is crisis-driven and drama-driven? First, **assess whether the problem is real or exaggerated.** If it is a real problem, and you can help, by all means, do so. If you can't help but know about resources or people who can help, provide the information they need to solve the problem. If it is exaggerated or is something that they can easily handle themselves, refrain from getting involved. This may also discourage them from trying to pull you in from future situations.

Second, **keep drama-prone people at a distance if you can.** There are times when you cannot keep them at a distance. That individual may be a spouse, family member, co-worker, friend, or someone you work with as part of an organization you are involved with. However, when you can stay away, do so, if only for your mental well-being.

Third, **don't approach drama-prone people about things that stir up drama-driven situations.** If you know something you say or do will provoke a crisis or drama-driven response, don't engage in that conversation or that behavior. If the behavior happens around a certain individual, don't bring that person around.

Finally, **walk away from the drama.** Recognize that walking away can be very difficult. There are often factors that make you feel that you should stay. There are emotional connections that may keep you from severing your ties. It can be hard to walk away, but if it gets to the place where the situation has an impact on your well-being, it is time to walk away. The question is, are you strong enough to walk away?

MPOWERED ME NEXT STEPS

S – Scripture – Read Psalm 1 out loud.

O – Observation – What do you notice about the verses? What do you think the main message is? What verses, words, or ideas jump out to you?

A – Application – Ask God how he wants you to apply the verse to your life.

P – Prayer – Pray for yourself and/or for others.

Chapter Reflection: Drama

_____

_____

_____

_____

_____

_____

To go deeper into this topic, please refer to **The Journal Workbook. **

10

PEOPLE PLEASER

Now, do you think I am trying to make people accept me? No, God is the one I am trying to please. Am I trying to please people? If I wanted to please people, I would not be a servant of Christ.
(Galatians 1:10, ERV)

"Don't go into the business of pleasing people. You can't please everybody. Simply do your best at what you do."
– Bangambiki Habyarimana, The Great Pearl of Wisdom

When you ask about a person who is a people pleaser, you will often hear descriptions such as nice, helpful, and giving. They are usually seen as someone who is always willing to do for others. When someone is in a bind, they can always be counted on to help when asked. They are reliable and can be counted on when others need them.

On the surface, being a people pleaser does not seem to be a bad thing. Being helpful when someone needs your help is a good thing. However, the motive behind people pleasing generally does not come from a positive place. People pleasers act typically due to a fear of rejection. They consciously or subconsciously believe, "If I don't do this thing for this person or these people, they will no longer like me, they might leave me, or they will no longer love me."

Another related impetus for people pleasing is fear of the consequences of disappointing someone or some people. It is a conscious or unconscious belief: "If I don't do this, I will disappoint him, her, or them. And then I will be punished, cast aside, or abandoned. Therefore, I people-please so I am not rejected, I don't disappoint others, and avoid any negative consequences."

There are potential mental and physical impacts to people pleasing. People pleasers are more likely to find themselves in toxic relationship patterns. People pleasers are more likely to remain in emotionally abusive relationships. People pleasers can become resentful, stressed, and depressed. People pleasers may also experience physical symptoms such as neck and shoulder soreness, headaches, muscle aches and tightness, shallow breathing, heart palpitations, throat constrictions, stomach aches, and tightness.

How can you know if you are a people pleaser? Take an inventory of how many of these identifying factors apply to you.

1. You don't know how to say no when others ask you to do things for them, even when you know you should say no.

2. You keep your opinions and feelings to yourself and

allow others to make decisions for you that you should make yourself.

3. It bothers you a lot if you find out that someone doesn't like you.

4. You are angry toward someone you work for or assist, and you don't understand why.

5. You cannot complete what you promise on time or put aside things you need to do to finish something for someone else.

Many people pleasers believe that what they are doing is being kind to others. They want to be seen as unselfish and as a good person. However, they often get taken advantage of by others. If you have someone in your life who is only with you or only hangs around you because of what you do for them, you should remove this from your circle of people you keep close to. This is a one-sided relationship; good relationships are usually reciprocal.

So, how do you stop being a people pleaser? First, **accept the fact that you cannot say yes to everyone and everything.** It is all right to say, "No." True friends and the people who care about you will not stop caring or will not abandon you because you say no. Be honest with yourself about what you can and cannot do, and don't feel obligated to do things you cannot do. I promise you that the people you say no will find another way to get it done.

Second, **learn to be less dependent on the validation of others in order for you to feel good about yourself.** Do more of the things that make you feel good about yourself. Associate with people who appreciate you, make you feel good about yourself, and don't expect you to do anything for them. Make a list of those things that make you special, and read that list to yourself every day as a reminder. If you love you, then you won't need the approval of others to feel loved.

Third, **eliminate those people from your life who only want things from you and can never do anything for you.** Some people don't add any value to your life. They have you around because the things you do add value to their lives. Why do you still keep them close? Remember that you are made in the image of God. You are special, not because of what you do, but simply because God made you that way.

Think about the stressors in your life. Are any of them caused by the pressure of trying to be pleasing to others? Depression, stress, and anxiety take a toll on your physical and mental health. Recognize if you are experiencing any of the above, go and get the help you need. A good counselor can provide you with the tools you need to deal with people pleasing.

MPOWERED ME NEXT STEPS

S – Scripture – Read Galatians 1:6-10 out loud.

O – Observation – What do you notice about the verses? What do you think the main message is? What verses, words, or ideas jump out to you?

A – Application – Ask God how he wants you to apply the verse to your life.

P – Prayer – Pray for yourself and/or for others.

Chapter Reflection: People Pleaser

_____

_____

_____

_____

_____

_____

To go deeper into this topic, please refer to **The Journal Workbook**.

Isaiah 26:3 (NIV):
"You will keep in perfect peace those whose minds
are steadfast, because they trust in you."

11

THE PACKED JAR

"Be careful not to spend your time having parties
and getting drunk or worrying about this life. If
you do that, you won't be able to think straight,
and the end might come when you are not ready."
(Luke 21:34)

"You have to relax when shooting an arrow. You can't be
tense. And that just helps in your day-to-day life"
-Stephen Amell

A well-known story is found in various forms on the internet. It is called by many names, but it has to do with a jar and various things placed in that jar. It begins with a professor who stands in front of his class with an empty jar. He fills it with stones, then asks the students, "Is this jar full?" The students looked at the jar and agreed that it was full.

The professor proceeded to grab some marbles and poured the marbles into the jar. He began to shake the jar, and the students watched as the marbles found their way into open spaces existing between the stones. He asks the students again, "Is this jar full?" There was a slight hesitation, but most of the students responded. "Yes, it is full."

The professor bent down, picked up a bag of sand, and began to pour sand into the jar. The sand filled the crevices and gaps left between the stones and the marbles. When the sand reached the top of the jar, the professor stopped and asked the students a third time, "Is this jar full?"

The students hesitated, and muffled expressions of "yes" and "no" were heard throughout the classroom. The professor reached out, picked up a jar of water, and poured water into the jar. The students watched as the sand absorbed the water. Finally, he reached the top of the jar, looked up, and asked, "Is the jar finally full?" Hesitantly, the students responded, "Yes?" The professor responds, "Yes, it is now full."

The story of the jar is a metaphor for our lives. There are some valuable lessons we need to remember. First, **you can take on a lot of things; choose wisely.** We are all allotted the same amount of time as everyone else. Our choices about what we do with the time we are given are unchangeable. Do-overs are not available. If we make bad decisions with our use of time, we can't go back and rewrite or redo that section of our lives. Spend your time on those things that have real value and meaning to you. Do things that make you better or bring about a better life.

Second, **remember to take time to relax and exhale.** If you are not careful, you will be in constant motion, and you will not take the time to smell the roses, engage with family and friends, rest, and recharge. I have never met anyone on their deathbed and wished they worked or partied more. Make the important people and things in your life your priority – that includes you. Take care of yourself.

Third, **if you discover that you have lost focus, unpack your jar and fill it with what matters.** You are not stuck with the jar that you have currently filled. You can empty your jar and fill it with new things. You can even discard your jar and its contents, get a new one, and start filling it again. The choice is yours. It's never too late.

MPOWERED ME NEXT STEPS

S – Scripture – Read Luke 21:34-36 out loud.
O – Observation – What do you notice about the verses? What do you think the main message is? What verses, words, or ideas jump out to you?
A – Application – Ask God how he wants you to apply the verse to your own life.
P – Prayer – Pray for yourself and/or for others.

Chapter Reflection: People Pleaser

_____

_____

_____

_____

_____

_____

***To go deeper into this topic, please refer to* **The Journal Workbook**.**

12

TRANSFORMATION

And Jacob sent messengers before him to Esau his brother in the land of Seir, the country of Edom, instructing them, "Thus you shall say to my lord Esau: Thus says your servant Jacob, 'I have sojourned with Laban and stayed until now. I have oxen, donkeys, flocks, male servants, and female servants. I have sent to tell my lord, in order that I may find favor in your sight.'" (Genesis 32:3-5, ESV)

"When things change inside you, things change around you."
Unknown

The early part of Jacob's life was one of trickery and deceit. Some writers conclude that this was such a recognized aspect of his character he was given a name that could be translated as "trickster" or "con man." He convinced his brother to give up his birthright, and he tricked his father into giving him the blessing reserved for the oldest child, his brother Esau. Jacob and his mother feared Esau's threats to murder Jacob, so she sent him away to her brother, in a place called Haram, until Esau's anger against Jacob subsided.

In Haram, in the home of his uncle Laban, Jacob learned a valuable life lesson: no matter how good of a con man you are, you will one day cross paths with someone who can out-con you. Jacob meets the daughter of Laban, Rachel, and falls in love. He agrees to work seven years for the hand of Rachel in marriage.

He works the agreed upon seven years, has a marriage ceremony and celebration, and consummates the marriage, only to discover that he had been tricked by his uncle. The woman he married was not his beloved Rachel but rather Rachel's older sister, Leah. When he confronts Laban, Laban tells him that the youngest cannot marry before the oldest. If he wants Rachel as well, he can work seven more years, and then Rachel can also be his.

Jacob works seven more years for Laban and takes the hand of Rachel in marriage. Jacob resorted to his ways and orchestrated things to end up with many servants and livestock. Years later, after leaving his parents empty-handed, he is married, has children, and is a wealthy man.

Jacob reaches a point where he feels the need to be a better man. He decides to return home and seek reconciliation with his brother, Esau. He gathers his family, servants, and livestock and begins the journey back to his homeland. On the way to meet his brother, he has an encounter with an angel. He battles with the angel and holds his own in the battle, but his hip becomes disjointed. Nevertheless, he holds on to the angel and declares, *"I will not let you go unless you bless me"* (Genesis 32:27).

The angel relents, provides Jacob with the blessing he seeks, and he gives him a new name, Israel. He explains this by saying, *"Your name shall no longer be called Jacob, but Israel, for you have striven with God and with men, and have prevailed"* (Genesis 32:28). So, Jacob, who is now called Israel, continues his quest to meet and reconcile with his brother. However, he is no longer the same person; his experiences have transformed him.

There are several lessons we can learn from the story of Jacob that we need to remember about trying to bring about change in someone else. First, **for transformation to occur, there must be a desire for change**, and that desire must come from the individual who needs change. No matter how hard you try, you cannot change someone who doesn't feel they need to change. You only have two choices: accept them as they are or frustrate yourself as you try to get them to change. The only person you have the power to change is you.

Second, **transformation always begins from the inside out.** Before you start to see external evidence of change in an individual, something must happen within. What they are doing may bother you, but it works for them – otherwise, they wouldn't continue doing it. Until something happens in their life that makes the status quo unacceptable, they will keep being who they are and doing what they do.

Third, **transformation sometimes requires you to right your wrongs.** This may not be the case in every situation, but sometimes, there are people we need to reconcile with or apologize and make restitution to before we can move on with our lives. It is a good idea to evaluate our lives and make sure that as we look to become a reflection of our best selves, there isn't anyone or anything we need to address.

MPOWERED ME NEXT STEPS

S – Scripture – Read Genesis 32:1-6 out loud.

O – Observation – What do you notice about the verses? What do you think the main message is? What verses, words, or ideas jump out to you?

A – Application – Ask God how he wants you to apply the verse to your life.

P – Prayer – Pray for yourself and/or for others.

Chapter Reflection: Transformation

_____

_____

_____

_____

_____

_____

To go deeper into this topic, please refer to **The Journal Workbook**.

CONCLUSION

Wow, congratulations on completing the Mpowered Me Mindset Reset! I know it must be overwhelming to feel both drained and excited simultaneously. You should be proud of yourself for pushing through tough obstacles and identifying areas of improvement. This program was designed to help you heal and grow, so take some time to reflect on your progress and meet with your accountability partner to discuss your journey. Remember, it's okay to redo the program and continue making progress. Take a moment to celebrate your accomplishments!

My goal is to inspire you to embark on a mindset reset that can establish a successful foundation for your business, ministry, or any aspect of your life. With our previous work on addressing negative emotions and thought patterns, let us now focus on cultivating positive practices that can lead to success. I urge you to stay on the path of positivity and witness the transformative power of God in your life.

www.MpoweredMe.com

RESOURCES

Admin. (2023, May 19). Genesis 50 : Jacob's funeral [English ERV bible]. Tamil ERV Bible. https://www.tamilervbible.in/genesis-50/

Adminimm. (2023, May 12). Depression - what is it? Integrative Medicine for Mental Health. https://immh2020.com/depression-what-is-it-4/

Bashirov, E. (2023, January 20). 5G nr initial access: How does a device establish connection with a cellular operator? MINTS. https://b5g-mints.eu/blog34/

bhidajat88, oleh. (2020, October 16). 12 rules of a simple life. Budi hidajat. https://budihidajat.com/2018/09/18/12-rules-of-simple-life/

Called to live in freedom. Down an Unfamiliar Road. (2020, May 12). https://rseyda38.net/2020/05/12/called-to-live-in-freedom-266/

Dr. Sajeev Dev, & Dr. Sajeev Dev. (2022, November 20). The true mark of maturity. Dr. Sajeev Dev. https://sajeevdev.com/the-true-mark-of-maturity/

Entente Dream. (2022, September 12). Dream of winning the lottery (Spiritual Meanings & interpretation). Entente Dream. https://www.ententechicago.com/dream-of-winning-the-lottery/

Genesis 32:3. Genesis 32:3 ESV - My Bible. (n.d.). https://mybible.com/bibles/esv/books/gen/chapters/32/verses/3

Genesis 32:5. Genesis 32:5 ESV - My Bible. (n.d.). https://mybible.com/bibles/esv/books/gen/chapters/32/verses/5

IndiStatus.com. (2023, August 17). Sometimes, when I say: I'm okay. I want someone to look me in the eyes, hug me tight, and say: I know you're not. IndiStatus.com. https://www.indistatus.com/quote/1829

Inspiringquotes.us. (2023, August 1). Quotes. Inspiring Quotes. https://www.inspiringquotes.us/author/6203-josephine-hart

Jared Dees. (n.d.). September 2020. Jared Dees. https://jareddees.com/2020/09/

Love the lord's teachings. www.FaithfulLamb.com. (n.d.). https://faithfullamb.com/bible-stories/june-11th-2020

Patience And Understanding In A Time Of Crisis. Denver Open Media. (n.d.). https://www.denveropenmedia.org/shows/patience-understanding-time-crisis says:, B., says:, T. A. T., & says:, L. (2017, March 24).

Wrestling with God. Dawn Ponderings. http://ponderings.theskeltons.org/2012/02/11/wrestling-with-god/

Scazzero, P. (2017). Emotionally healthy spirituality - It's Impossible To Be Spiritually Mature, Zondervan.

Staff, Y. (n.d.). Genesis 37:18-36 When they saw him from a distance and before he came close to them, they plotted against him to put him to death. they said to one another, "Here comes this dreamer! now then, come and let us kill him: New American standard bible - NASB 1995 (NASB1995): Download the bible app now. YouVersion | The Bible App | Bible.com. https://www.bible.com/bible/100/GEN.37.18-36

Steven Wiegand blog. (n.d.). https://www.stevewiegand.com/index.php/2016/06/04/there-comes-a-time-in-your-life-when-you-walk-away-from-all-the-drama-and-people-who-create-it-you/

The story: A victorious limp. already & not yet. (2013, February 15). https://jasonbybee.com/2013/02/15/the-story-a-victorious-limp/

Taylor, E. J. (n.d.). What do I say? Talking with patients about spirituality. Templeton Foundation Press, ©2007.

Team, B. (2023, April 7). How to deal with travel anxiety: Babylon health us. Babylon Health. https://www.babylonhealth.com/en-us/blog/health/how-to-deal-with-travel-anxiety

Understanding soap for beginners bible worksheet. Free Bible Worksheets. (2022, August 27). https://freebibleworksheets.com/printables/understanding-soap-for-beginners-bible-worksheet/

Why does it hurt so much? Rejoice. (2023, March 11). https://rejoiceministries.org/why-does-it-hurt-so-much/

ABOUT THE AUTHOR

Natasha Richards is a powerhouse of faith and motherhood, driven by a fierce desire to empower people and organizations with practical applications of God's word. With her powerful message of personal transformation, this pastor and author is on a mission to help you unlock your full potential today. Join her on this journey of self-discovery and growth, and start living the life you've always dreamed of. Learn more about her programs and resources at *www. MpoweredMe.com.*

MORE BOOKS
FROM NATASHA RICHARDS

Mindset Reset: The Journal Workbook

Go deeper into the transformation power with *The Mindset Reset Journal Workbook.* This companion book is your key to unlocking positive transformation and reaching your full potential.

ISBN: 979-8-9894494-0-8

You can purchase this book on Amazon, Barnes & Noble and everywhere books are sold.

For the Levites: A Closer Walk with Jesus Beyond the Music

For the Levites, is a devotional and prayer journal for ministers of music. It is divided into four sections: your journey, your fruits, your purpose and commitment to ministry. As you embark on these days of prayer, go beyond the music and have a closer walk with God.

ISBN: 978-1-948877-49-7

You can purchase this book on Amazon, Barnes & Noble and everywhere books are sold.

www.ingramcontent.com/pod-product-compliance
Lightning Source LLC
Chambersburg PA
CBHW060351130626
46553CB00003B/1185